Highlights® Handbook

Nature's Wonderful Family

Edited by Jack Myers, Ph.D.

Illustrated by Robert C. Kray

The Porcupine
A Bristling Armory

By A. A. Howe

One of the strangest of nature's woodland curiosities is our friend Porky.

He rattles when he walks and backs up to attack! He is a harmless, slow-footed beast that mutters to himself. But how fearful he looks! How fearful he is to handle! Placidly, he saunters through the underbrush without concern. Nature has endowed him with enough weapons to kill a mountain lion. He is a match for the big-footed lynx and the red-toothed wolverine.

Porky, sometimes mistakenly called hedgehog, is really the Canadian porcupine. He lives in the northeastern part of the United States and in Canada. One of his favorite haunts is in the forests of the Adirondack Mountains.

Porky is a chunky, blunt-faced rodent about 2½ feet long, weighing 15 to 25 pounds. He has a short tail, some 6 inches long, which is very muscular and powerful. In addition to the long, soft hairs that cover his body, sharp, needle-like quills sprout from head, back, and tail. When he is aroused, these quills rise; and Porky becomes a bristling armory.

The quills are hollow little tubes, pointed at the ends and lightly attached to his skin. The slightest touch will remove them. These remarkable quills are fitted with numberless little barbs like the barbs on fishhooks. When a pointed quill penetrates the warm body of a victim, it swells up. Because of the barbs, it can move only toward its point so it keeps forcing itself deeper into the flesh with every twinge of muscle the victim makes.

Thus many a porcupine has avenged his own death weeks after he has been eaten, because his attacker has also been the victim of the quills which slowly work themselves in deeper and deeper.

In spite of his bristling armor of quills, Porky has a weak spot—his nose. A hard blow with a stick on the tip of his sensitive nose will kill him.

Big cats will hunt Porky only if forced to. Often it is a fatal choice. Foxes, wolves, wildcats, mountain lions, and even bears have been found dead in the forest with quills in them.

If attacked, Porky follows a set routine. He tucks his head under a log to protect his delicate nose and, with feet close together, hugs the ground to guard his underside. Then he raises his quills. This makes Porky look twice his size. Next, he clicks his teeth, makes a grumbling noise, and wags his tail from side to side. When this occurs, a wise enemy will leave Porky alone; but if curiosity gets the better of him and he comes still closer, Porky will vigorously wag his tail. If the attacker has gotten too close, he is likely to get a face full of those needle-sharp quills which will send him screaming in pain back to the safety of the forest. If the attacker still persists after this onslaught,

Porky will stab his enemy with quills by moving back and forth as he backs up to the nearest tree. Then he clumsily lumbers up the tree and calmly starts chewing on bark or twigs as if nothing had happened.

The violent lashing of his stout tail when he is provoked loosens the lightly attached quills. But Porky cannot "throw" his quills as has sometimes been claimed. The ten or twenty quills Porky has lost in an encounter do not worry him a bit. In a few months they will grow back, and he has some 30,000 in his arsenal.

Porky lives in a hollow log or a cavern among rocks. He sleeps in safety, curled up, his spiny back toward the entrance. On the coldest days, Porky sleeps; but at every thaw he crawls from his den and climbs into treetops, where he stuffs himself with green bark—often killing the tree. He feeds mostly at night. A lazy creature, Porky travels no farther than he has to, sometimes remaining in two or three trees for a whole season. He has a great fondness for tender young twigs and has discovered a way to enjoy them to the fullest. He pulls several slender branches carefully together so they will bear his weight. Then he goes out on them as far as he dares, and with his

powerful paws bends back their ends toward himself in an upward arc and passes the sweet green twig tips slowly through his mouth, somewhat in the manner of a man eating corn on the cob!

Porky goes freely about by day in his bristly armor. He may dawdle in the same tree all day if he likes the bark. When he ambles through the underbrush he mutters to himself—he sniffs, squeaks, chatters, and even grunts.

Slow-witted, homely old Porky is also clumsy, but nature has given him built-in protection. If he should fall into the water, he has no cause for concern because his hollow, air-filled quills keep him afloat like a bobbing cork! Should he fall out of a tree, his quills cushion the shock, and he placidly goes on his way.

Porky has other peculiarities. Sometimes he will sit in a tree and let out a long, loud wail or scream to himself for a whole hour or more for no apparent reason.

Another oddity about Porky is a strange mania for salt. This habit is most exasperating to campers and woodsmen. Should Porky venture into camp, he will eat all the butter he can find. If there is none, he may eat an empty wooden bowl if there are traces of salt in it. And he will chew up ax handles and canoe paddles because of the salty trace of

sweat on them. A forest ranger once left his car to go up to his fire station, forgetting to close the window. When he returned a week later, he found that Porky had chewed off the wooden steering wheel. Only the metal spokes remained! Woodsmen have been awakened at night by Porky's clamor, and have discovered him eating sticks of dynamite!

Porky's worst enemy is man; but the fisher, a weasel-like animal, sometimes is able to seize Porky by the throat where he is least protected by quills, turn him over on his back, and bite him fatally.

Porky mates in October, and the youngsters are born in April. Amazingly, the babies are larger than bear cubs at birth, measuring over 11 inches long. But what is even more astonishing is the fact that the babies are born with quills a half-inch long. How such babies could be delivered has puzzled many people. The truth is, the young at birth are surrounded by a very tough membrane, which protects the mother.

No creature in nature has been supplied with greater protection than Porky, but nature has given him more—a peculiar personality!

Little Kids and Big Goats

By Gertrude McCafferty

When you see a nimble little goat at your zoo, don't you think it would make a fine pet? You are right! A young goat, known as a kid, is a lively, playful animal. It is ever ready to scamper and run. My youngsters, Jeanne and Bob, used to say a goat liked to play king-of-the-hill by taking possession of a box or a high spot, and repelling invaders.

We first became acquainted with goats when a business friend, a Swiss, found we had moved into a country home with five acres.

"You should have a goat," he told us. "It has been said that they were revered by Mohammed and Buddha. They believed that a household having a goat was blessed. With three goats, they were thrice blessed. And the Irish family has a goat to keep the banshees away and the leprechauns dancing on the lawn."

Before long we received a white goat, a Saanen, which we named Blanche (French for white). Then our friend decided the white goat needed a companion, and we received a brown-and-white beauty, a Toggenburg. The deerlike Toggenburg is all brown with white stripes up each side of its face and white socks on its four ankles. These two breeds, the Saanen and the Toggenburg, are Swiss breeds and are named for the valleys in which they originated. They have alert ears and pert, turned-up tails like deer.

We had much to learn about goats. We had thought of them as animals which butt people and rummage through dumps, eating tin cans. We soon found they would not dispose of our tin cans. They had gained that reputation from ill-fed animals nibbling paper labels.

Our new animals, and the young kids which came after, proved entirely different from those old tales. They delighted us with their friendliness. Their quickness in action and thinking won our respect. They did butt, but it was a playful gesture. And none of the animals failed to respond to kind treatment.

Our goats are clean animals. They will not drink stale water. As my daughter Jeanne used to say about her pet, "Tillie doesn't like to drink after the other goats." Keen senses tell them when another animal has had a drink from the container. Fussy goats will snort disdainfully at offerings of leftovers.

Jeanne learned the goats' habits quickly. "Tillie won't eat the apple I dropped," she told me. "And she does like apples and peaches, but she doesn't like dirty food. None of our goats do."

She was right about that. As fond as they are of fruit, few of our pets would eat the leftover core. We found, however, that Tillie would eat Jeanne's apple core and Geraldine would eat mine. We decided it was a matter of the affection they had for us.

I received much of my information on goats from my observant youngsters. "They don't have upper-front teeth," Jeanne said. "They have a tough gum or upper palate. It is solid, too. Watch Tillie eat this thorny wild rose branch." Tillie downed it gracefully.

"They chew a cud like a cow,"

Nubian doe and kid

Toggenburg kid

"Did you know goats once lived in the White House?"

"Now, Bob," I chided.

"That's right. President Lincoln's son Tad had goats in the White House. A telegram from Lincoln said to tell Tad, 'Father and the goats are well, especially the goats.' A letter said that Nanny had been found resting in the middle of Tad's bed."

So look closely at the goats when next you see them. Can you find the barbell in their eyes? Are they chewing a cud? Guess where they lived before they became Americans. Watch them play king-of-the-hill. You will see they truly are friendly, playful animals.

Bob added. "See, they stand very still. Then they burp impolitely and their food comes back to their mouth. They chew it again."

Springtime was kid time. Baby goats started arriving from February until the one we named Liberty Belle, honoring her illustrious birth date, July 4th. None of the kids had horns at birth. But in a short time a few would develop little bumps which soon would be horns. Horns are dangerous to other animals, and they can be caught in fences. So we would apply a special caustic to halt the growth.

"Look into a goat's eyes at different times of the day," said Bob. "You will find their pupils change shape like a cat's eyes. Sometimes they will be round. Other times you will see a bar with a round ball on each end. It looks like a weight lifter's barbell."

The color of goats varies greatly, but thoroughbred animals are distinctive. Like cats and dogs, good goats are registered and numbered for generations. Registered animals are kept by goat dairies. Many good milk goats produce over six quarts of milk daily during peak season.

Like our immigrants, they came from all over the world. They arrived with our earliest settlers. A listing of stock at Jamestown in 1611 recorded one hundred goats. They have come from Switzerland and France and many other countries.

If you have seen a large, dark goat with floppy ears, you were looking at a Nubian. This oriental breed comes from Egypt, Ethiopia, and other North African countries.

Saanen kid

Which Does Not Belong?

1. Which one is not a swimmer?
   penguin   duck   chicken
2. Which one is not a mammal?
   whale   salmon   porpoise
3. Which one is not extinct?
   cougar   mammoth   dodo
4. Which one can fly?
   penguin   ostrich   vulture
5. Which one is carnivorous (meat-eating)?
   Brontosaurus   Tyrannosaurus
   Stegosaurus
6. Which one does not lay eggs?
   turtle   porcupine   platypus
7. Which one is poisonous?
   kingsnake   water snake   copperhead
8. Which one is active at night?
   cardinal   eagle   owl
9. Which is not a marsupial (animal with pouch)?
   opossum   weasel   kangaroo

Answers:

1.chicken 2.salmon 3.cougar 4.vulture 5.Tyrannosaurus 6.porcupine 7.copperhead 8.owl 9.weasel

5

Salmon
King of the North Pacific

By Cyrus M. McNeely

The silvery fish leaped to within a few inches of the top of the cascading water, then tumbled back. Time after time it jumped, until once it landed at the crest of the falls, slithered there for a moment, and with a final burst of energy zipped into the calm water above. I let out my breath and found that I was winded after this wonderful show of nature. But what was this brave and handsome fish? Why, it was a salmon, king of the North Pacific!

Salmon are noble creatures that roam the deep, blue waters of the North Pacific Ocean. Their behavior and bodies are designed to meet every challenge in an exciting and dangerous life. They begin this life, however, not in the ocean, but in the bottom of streams, often hundreds of miles from the sea. By scientists, salmon are called **anadromous** fish—they are born in fresh water, mature in the sea, and return to fresh water to produce their young. Their life history is quite a story, and I would like to tell you about it.

In the spring, salmon eggs hatch, and in a few weeks the young fish begin to wriggle from the gravel and rocks in the bed of a stream which runs toward the Pacific Ocean. Sometimes, when I am digging in a stream bottom, I see these tiny, pink, squirming creatures in the shovel. They are **alevins**—young salmon with part of the salmon eggs still attached. If I had not dug them up, they would have come out by themselves in a few days.

After escaping the gravel, some species of salmon (there are five different species) go immediately to sea, some go into a lake on the stream system, and some stay in the stream for a period of time to feed and grow.

In the stream their narrow, streamlined bodies allow them to feed in swift currents on tiny plants and animals. To rest, they swim into quiet, sheltered parts of the stream. If you are near a known salmon stream in the spring or summer, sneak up on them in the shallow pools behind stumps and logs near the shore, and watch them dart about between pool and riffle. Gently throw some bread crumbs on the water, and observe the fish frolic and fight for them. These young, growing salmon are called **fry**.

When the fry are a little more than a year old, and four to six inches long, they become silvery and prepare for their migration to the sea. They are called **smolts** when they leave for the ocean with some of the first high waters of their second spring.

Now, the sea is like a pasture, vast in extent and rich in food, and the salmon roam and feed in it until they are mature. Depending upon species, this may take from two to five years. On the high sea they are pursued by commercial and sport fishermen as well as larger fish and mammals. If they compete well and survive, they will swim thousands of miles and grow to as much as fifty pounds before returning to fresh water.

It is during this return trip that the remarkable abilities of the salmon really stand out. Perhaps the most astonishing thing is their ability to find the stream of their birth. This "homing instinct" has long stumped fishery scientists, but it can probably be explained as a form of sensitivity to the different smells and chemicals in the various waters. Whatever it is, it serves an important purpose: It makes sure that salmon come year after year to all suitable streams.

During the upstream dash to the spawning grounds, the streamlined bodies of the salmon play their most important role. Stream courses are often partly blocked by low water, falls, rapids, cataracts, and cascades. Sometimes man-made barriers such as dams completely block streams. In order to survive all these obstacles, salmon must be powerful and fast swimmers, and tremendous jumpers with great endurance. Once in a tiny mountain creek I watched a large salmon slowly beating its way up through very fast, shallow water that came less than halfway up its sides. It could barely breathe, and it often became stuck on rocks. I wanted to get down in the water to help it.

While I could not do much more than cheer for that particular fish, scientists and engineers have developed ways to help schools of salmon get around some impassable falls and dams. One of the best of these is the fish ladder. A fish ladder is usually a trough of water separated into pools by concrete walls. It extends around a dam from the lower side to the higher side, and fish swim from pool to pool through a slot or hole in the wall.

Mature salmon undergo a series of bodily changes in preparation for spawning on their way upstream. The male becomes bright red, and may develop a hump and an ugly snout with sharp teeth. The female changes to a lighter shade of red. In both sexes the reproductive organs develop. You might see these colorful spawners from August through December in the same stream in which you watched the fry earlier.

Once at the ancestral spawning ground, the female digs a nest in the stream bottom with her large fanlike tail. When the nest is formed, she lays her eggs in it as the male fertilizes them. Then she uses her tail again to bury them deep in the stream bed where they will incubate a few months before hatching.

The long journey upstream has left the beautiful bodies of the salmon beaten and scarred. In a small stream far up in the mountains, I saw a male salmon that had finished spawning. It had scarcely any fins or tail left, and even one eye was gone. It looked terrible, but it had fought and survived to complete its life history. I watched as it lay in the still, quiet waters near the bank, waiting to die as all Pacific salmon must after spawning. It would never see its young, but it had made sure that there would be a new generation of kings of the North Pacific.

sockeye spawning

The Armadillo
A Live Tank

R.C.Kray

By Dorothy Sharp Carter

How would you like to have an army of small armored tanks—live ones—wandering around your backyard? And doing things ordinary tanks can't do, such as burrowing into the earth till they're completely hidden or halfway curling up (Can you imagine a real tank doing that?) or apparently sucking up ants and spiders and scorpions as fast as a vacuum cleaner.

Well, that's what we have on our ranch in Texas. Of course, they're not really tanks; they're nine-banded armadillos, small animals related to the anteater. Their fancy scientific name is *Dasypus novemcinctus*, meaning "rough footed with nine bands."

The early Spanish explorers who first saw them in Mexico in the sixteenth century gave them the name armadillo, meaning "little armored thing."

A nine-banded armadillo is from two to three feet long when full-grown and weighs about thirteen pounds. Half of his length is his long, thin tail which is made up of layers of scaly rings. His body is covered by a grayish-brown sheath ridged by nine bands around the middle. His head, which is small and long with rabbit-like ears, can be pulled back under this armor, the way a turtle can retreat into his shell. His feet have long, sharp claws which he uses for digging and

for defending himself.

The armadillo eats a varied diet of roots, worms, reptiles, snails, berries, and small mammals. Unfortunately, he also relishes tomatoes and melons—which makes him unpopular with gardeners. But insects are his favorite food. He can pick them up with his long, prehensile—That's a word for you to look up—tongue, similar to an anteater's. Then he chews them with his back teeth. He has no front teeth to bite with.

The armadillo is a creature of slow, leisurely habits. Often I have watched him saunter along, rooting under stones and into leaves, looking for his favorite food—such as ants—in no hurry at all.

In hard stony areas he lives among rocks or in thickets. In regions where the soil is soft, he digs a burrow—or rather, quite a few burrows. These are from four to twenty-five feet in length; the nest chamber is usually about five feet below the surface. The nest is lined with grasses and leaves. From time to time he carries out this bedding and brings in fresh grasses, like a tidy housekeeper. Other animals such as raccoons, rabbits, and skunks probably make use of his burrows while he is away. I read that a skunk was once seen entering an armadillo's burrow. A while later the armadillo appeared and entered the same burrow. Soon after, up came the skunk and wandered off—not angry, not upset. So I suppose the armadillo was polite in seeing off his guest. But he did see him off—no invitation to stay the night. Armadillos are sociable, at least to other armadillos, and sometimes can be found feeding in quite large groups.

The home range of an armadillo is about eight acres, but he does not have a marked individual range as birds do. He cannot live in places that have long periods of freezing weather, maybe because of a scarcity of insects.

Young armadillos are born in March, usually four at a time but sometimes more. The litter consists of all brothers or all sisters, never both in one litter. They are born open-eyed, and their armor is soft, like leather, until they grow older. The life span of the armadillo is about four years.

The armadillo has a very clever trick for crossing bodies of water. To cross a small stream he simply walks along the bottom. But to traverse a wider stream he takes in great breaths of air to inflate himself. Then, like an armored beachball, he manages to swim across with only his small snout showing. He doesn't seem to enjoy swimming, but he does like to wallow in mud.

The armadillo's main enemies are men, dogs, coyotes, and wild pigs. His defense is running or burrowing. He can out-dodge most dogs and his armor allows him to escape into a thorny thicket. He is quick at burrowing and can dig himself out of sight in a couple of minutes if the ground is soft enough. Once "dug in," he is hard to get out, even by pulling on his tail, for his ridged sheath acts to hook him into the ground. Usually the armadillo will curl up only when he is exhausted or injured. He prefers to run.

His sight and hearing are poor but are compensated for by a good sense of smell. I have photographed an armadillo from as close as four feet. I was upwind from him, and he neither saw nor heard me. Quite contented, he went on with his rooting.

When he does sense danger, the armadillo tends to rear up on his hind legs, braced by his tail, to sniff the air. This habit of jumping upward when startled can be disastrous. An automobile, which might straddle him, will hit him as he jumps or rears up.

Man is probably his worst enemy. For a time armadillos were blamed for the disappearance of quail and were hunted widely. Later it was discovered that herds of goats and sheep were eating away the brush and foliage of the quails' cover, causing the birds to move away. The armadillos were not to blame after all.

The little animal is valuable in a number of ways. He destroys harmful insects. His rooting leaves small holes in the ground which help to cultivate the soil.

Thousands of years ago relatives of the armadillo roamed the Americas. Some of these were called *Glyptodon*, and they were a good deal larger than our present-day armadillo. Casts of *Glyptodon* shells may be seen in museums. Today giant armadillos, some five feet long, live in Brazil.

In early Texas history the armadillo was found only along the Mexican border, but he has slowly traveled northward. As late as 1890 the animal was considered unusual in central Texas. By 1925 he had reached Louisiana. And at present he can be found through most of Texas into Oklahoma and east to Mississippi and Florida. His population is on the increase, and probably only a dislike of cold weather keeps him from spreading throughout the whole country.

Too bad he can't. We could do a lot worse than have a countryful of such harmless, helpful little "tanks."

Elephants

The elephant is the largest of the land animals. He is a huge fellow, weighing six or seven tons. (The blue whale is the largest animal that ever lived, weighing at least seventy-five tons. But he is a sea animal.)

Doubtless, to most people the trunk of the elephant is his outstanding feature. But to the elephant himself, his trunk is far more than a source of wonder. It is his most prized possession, for there seems to be no end to the useful things he can do with it.

He can use it as a weapon with which to whack an enemy or to spank an elephant-child who is getting into mischief. With it he can bring food and water to his mouth, and give himself a dust bath or a refreshing shower bath when he finds welcome water after a long, hard trek. Also with his trunk he can smell and sniff—his keenest sense is that of smell. And with it he can let loose loud trumpet calls of anger or alarm that make the plains and jungles quiver.

This useful, tapering trunk is six to eight feet long and is an extension of the nose. It is a sort of fifth limb, strong enough to lift a heavy tree trunk, but with such a sensitive tip that it can pick up a blade of grass.

Elephants are gregarious, or social, animals—that is, they live in large-sized herds. The herd generally includes parents, brothers and sisters, uncles, aunts, and cousins by the dozens.

In Africa, where one kind of elephant lives, these herds wander through the forests and over the grassy plains and lowlands, searching for clean water which is one of their greatest needs. When they find it, they spend plenty of time enjoying it, drinking it and taking refreshing shower baths. In crossing a stream, the mother elephant supports her child in front of her with her trunk. In climbing steep places, she shoves it from behind. The herd usually travels single file, the mother elephants going ahead of the young ones, but not too fast for them to keep up. If alarmed, the male elephants may hurry on ahead, but the mothers stay with their children. Often the mother elephant affectionately fondles her child with her trunk. But the father elephants don't pay much attention to the little ones.

Wild elephants prefer browsing to grazing, and they are especially fond of green leaves, tender shoots of plants, and the soft bark of trees. If coveted shoots of a tree are beyond the reach of an elephant, he may push over the tree, even though it is a very large one, in order to get what he wants.

Wild elephants eat more than those in captivity. But even these have pretty big appetites. For instance, an elephant in a zoo or circus will eat about one hundred pounds of hay a day, in addition to rations of oats, bran, and vegetables and gifts of peanuts and buns from his admirers. If an elephant isn't feeling well, he will get an extra helping of salad vegetables. For him, a nice little drink means a gallon and a half of water.

Besides being the largest of the land animals, some authorities place the elephant at the head of all animals in intelligence. In any case, all authorities rank him high. And many remarkable instances are told of the wise ways of the wild elephant. In captivity he is easily trained, and not only learns quickly to obey his keeper but may form a strong affection for him. There is a saying that "an elephant never forgets." This may not be entirely true, but there is no doubt that he has a remarkable memory.

There are two main groups of elephants, the African and the Asian or Indian. African elephants are larger, stronger, and more fierce than those of Asia. The female, as well as the male, has long tusks. In the male these may be six to eight feet long. They are of ivory and are of great value. The Asian female has no tusks, or at least very small ones. There are other differences between these two groups, but the most easily noticed difference is in the ears. The African elephant has very large, floppy ears, while the ears of the Asian elephant are relatively small. If you ever see on television or in a book the picture of an elephant with large, floppy ears, you will know at once that he belongs to the African group.

African elephants are to be found over most of the African continent south of the Sahara Desert. Asian elephants are native to India, Ceylon, Pakistan, Burma, Indochina, Malaya, Sumatra, and Borneo.

Elephants, like all living creatures, have their own peculiarities. Here are some of them: The elephant's skin is very thick—it may be more than an inch thick, and yet it is so sensitive that flies or mosquitoes can drive the poor fellow to distraction. Elephants are very light sleepers and sleep only about half the time that a human being does. They usually sleep standing up. The tusks are almost entirely of ivory and keep growing as long as the elephant lives. His eyes are small, and the sight is poor. But his sense of smell is very keen, and he gathers needed information by sniffing. Wild elephants feed about sixteen to twenty-one hours each day. They may travel fifty to sixty miles a day if they are searching for clean water.

There are many other interesting things to know about elephants. And the more we learn about the ways of the elephant, the more we wonder at this amazing member of earth's family.

These facts were abstracted from *Elephants* by Richard Carrington, published by Basic Books, Inc., New York, and adapted by permission. The author is a Fellow of the Royal Anthropological Institute, the Royal Geographical Society, and the Zoological Society of London.

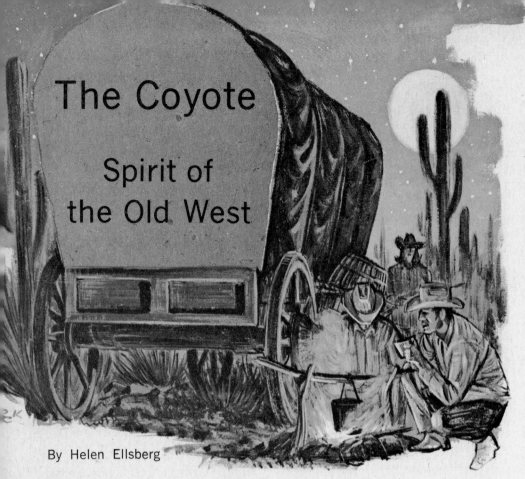

The Coyote

Spirit of the Old West

By Helen Ellsberg

The lean, tawny coyote resembles a small wolf and in some places is called the brush wolf. He has also been called "The Spirit of the Old West" because, like the pioneers who crossed the plains, he is tough, spunky, and self-reliant. He has not changed since those early days.

If you cross the plains and desert country today and camp beside a stream with your modern camping equipment, you will see no buffalo, no fighting cowboys and Indians. But as you climb into your sleeping bag and doze off, the long, quavering call you hear in the distance that makes the hair tingle along the back of your neck—the howl of a coyote—will be the same sound your forefathers heard as they "bedded down" in their covered wagons.

Because he is so shrewd and adaptable, the coyote has managed to survive where the buffalo, the passenger pigeon, the timber wolf, and many other North American wild creatures have been exterminated. The buffalo was a herd animal. They could not change their ways, and therefore were killed by the thousands. The coyote, too, once hunted in packs, but he learned the danger in this and became a lone hunter. Coyotes like each other's company and sometimes are seen "visiting" in little groups of three or four or even a half-dozen—often barking or howling together in a sort of wilderness glee club. They usually hunt alone but sometimes team up with one or two other coyotes and form "relays" to run down swifter animals such as the jackrabbit and antelope. But you will find no packs of coyotes where hunters could kill many of them at once.

Another reason the coyote survives is that he is adaptable in his eating habits. The great herds of buffalo could not exist today, even if hunters had not destroyed them, because the grassy plains have been plowed under and there would be nothing for them to eat. The coyote does not depend upon one food. He will catch rodents, rabbits, beetles, and grasshoppers. He will eat roots, seeds, berries, fruit, and watermelon. He will finish off the remains of a mountain lion's kill. He will catch minnows, frogs, and tadpoles in a stream or swamp. And, unfortunately, if he has a chance, he will steal a lamb or a fat chicken from a farmyard.

Because coyotes will prey upon domestic animals if they have a chance, man is trying to kill all of them off by trapping and by the use of a terrible poison called 1080. But modern man forgets what the Indians and Mexicans knew: When the balance of nature is upset, there is always trouble. Where the coyotes have been killed off, rats, mice, rabbits, and ground squirrels have multiplied by the thousands. These animals have caused more damage to crops and pastures than the coyotes ever did to sheep and chickens. Those who trapped and poisoned the coyotes because they killed sheep now find that they have not been so clever as they thought. The increasing rodents not only eat the grass but the grass seeds as well, so that no new grass grows and the land cannot feed as many sheep or cattle as it did before nature's balance was upset. As the grass dies out, the water table sinks lower and at last the land becomes dry and useless.

Wood rats and ground squirrels are even endangering a national park. Ecologists, studying many disturbing changes in our American environment, found that the great Saguaro National Monument in Arizona may be doomed because there are no coyotes to kill off the growing thousands of rodents who eat the giant cactus and kill the

12

plants which provide shade for the young saguaro plants.

The coyote is considered one of the most cunning of all animals, so cunning that it is often difficult to make sure that all the accounts about him are really true. The Indians of many tribes credited him with supernatural powers. They thought that any animal so very clever must have come from the spirit world. They often call him "Brother Coyote." In fact the word *coyote* comes to us from an Aztec word meaning sagacious.

Modern man has many wonderful inventions, but he is not nearly so wise as the Indians were when it comes to an understanding of nature. Most Apache and Navajo shepherds will never kill a coyote. Not only do they know that he does more good than harm, but they respect him for his cleverness, and their legends are full of tales about him.

Coyotes do many wise things. They burrow under a ground squirrel or gopher hole and as a result

they have ventilation. They do not line their dens with grass or straw in which fleas could live. A layer of dust on the bare den floor helps get rid of these pests.

They also seem to have a sense of humor. When chased by a dog, a coyote will sometimes start running in little circles. Then he keeps widening the circle until the dog suddenly finds that the coyote is chasing him! But the best-known trick, and one which I have twice observed, is to lead a dog on until he is out of sight of his master (who might have a gun), then turn on him and send him flying home. A coyote sometimes even has a friend or two waiting over the hill to help him out.

People who have studied them closely believe that the coyote does not make his barks, yaps, and howls by opening and closing his jaws the way dogs do. They believe that all the sound is made in the "voice box" (larynx) in somewhat the same manner that a ventriloquist speaks without moving his lips.

They go further and say that it is even possible that the coyote can "throw" his voice, somewhat as a ventriloquist does. If so, this would explain the fact that what often sounds like a dozen coyotes will turn out to be only one or two.

The coyote has the same mate for life. In the spring he helps dig the den and hunts food for the new family. When the pups are about two months old, their parents take them hunting. Usually at first grasshoppers and beetles are all they can catch. But soon they are catching ground squirrels and field mice. By fall they go hunting on their own and must find land unclaimed by other coyotes. Their biggest problems are to survive the first winter of hunting on their own and, later, to avoid traps and poisons.

More and more people are beginning to understand that the coyote is not a villain but has an important place in the society of nature. Hopefully, there will never be a time when his voice is stilled forever. It is sometimes weird and sad, sometimes lively and gay. But it is always wild and free—truly the spirit of the Old West.

The Opossum—
A Special Kind of Animal

By Julia F. Lieser

Mrs. Opossum doesn't have a hat to hang up, but if she did, that's where her home would be—for the time being. As it is, home for Mrs. Opossum is the coziest place she can find in which to curl up when the notion for a nap overtakes her.

Let's face facts—Mrs. Opossum is shiftless when it comes to housekeeping chores. Now that doesn't mean that she neglects her children. She does make a nest, or takes over somebody else's abandoned nest in a hollow tree, but even that is only temporary until the children are old enough to take care of themselves.

Mrs. Opossum isn't very bright, either. If all the animals were to take a test, she would turn up at the bottom of the list when the scores were marked. She cannot run fast and she has no defense. When caught or molested, she merely rolls onto one side and plays dead. Even when poked in the side or picked up and carried by her tail, she still continues to play dead.

Mrs. Opossum could never win any beauty prizes. In fact, she is downright homely. Her fur is coarse, and gray in color. Her face is white with rounded, black, hairless ears and coal-black eyes. She has a long snout like a pig, and a long, scaly, ratlike tail. She is about the size of a large house cat, with shorter legs and a stouter body.

Just what DOES Mrs. Opossum have? She is a special kind of animal, a **marsupial.** And the opossums are the only marsupials found in North America.

Marsupials are a class of animals that have pouches in which to carry their young. Kangaroos also have such pouches, but they are found only in Australia. When Mrs. Opossum's babies are born, five to fourteen in a litter, they are smaller than bees. A whole litter could fit into a teaspoon. They have tiny, sharp claws which they use to crawl up their mother's belly and into her pouch. They attach themselves to

nipples and remain there for two months or more. For another month they stay close to their mother, nursing when hungry.

When the babies are about the size of full-grown mice, they leave the pouch and crawl onto their mother's back, where they cling to her fur as she moves about, hunting for food. When their short legs are strong enough to hold up their stout bodies, they begin toddling alongside their mother.

At three months Mrs. Opossum weans her youngsters and teaches them to eat solid food. Opossums eat a variety of food, both animal and vegetable. They eat fruits, berries, insects, frogs, mice and small rodents. After eating, they sit on their hind legs and wash like a cat.

Mrs. Opossum has another unusual feature, a very skillful tail. She can wrap it around a tree branch, hang head-down, reach into a nest with her front paws, and steal the eggs. It also comes in handy when she is making a nest. She gathers weeds and grasses with her mouth and front paws, passes them under her belly, between her hind legs, and into a loop made with her tail. She then drags this nesting material along behind her.

You don't often see Mrs. Opossum because she is a night-loving animal. She sleeps all day and goes out at night to hunt for food. Mrs. Opossum doesn't migrate or hibernate when winter comes. She accepts winter for what it is, a time of hardship. She spends much of her time sleeping but may go forth to find a snack, even risking frostbite on her naked tail. Then she finds a cozy spot to sleep, in a hollow tree or under a rock, and curls up again. This is home for now. Perhaps tomorrow night she will find a better place.

The Albatross

By A. A. Howe

Have you ever heard of a bird that sleeps while it glides through the air? There is one, the albatross, and it is a very remarkable bird.

The albatross is a large sea bird, the largest of which is known as the wandering albatross. It is white in color but has black feathers on the tips of the wings and tail.

The wandering albatross has a heavy body, and long, narrow wings that are very strong. The wings, when spread, measure from six to twelve feet from tip to tip. Both the tail and legs are short, and the big webbed feet have no hind toe. The large, stout, hooked bill is covered with a hard, horny growth.

Most albatrosses live where the weather and oceans are cold. People who live inland or near the seashore seldom see an albatross because it spends most of its time flying over the ocean at great distances from land. Only sailors and passengers on ships far out at sea get to see this huge, graceful bird.

The wandering albatross is very powerful. It will follow a ship for days at a time without seeming to rest, but can settle on the water where it feeds on cuttlefish and squid. It has a very big appetite. After satisfying its hunger, the albatross is ready to fly again. But it does not rise out of the water like ducks or geese do. It has a most unusual way of getting into flight. Wings spread wide, the albatross seems to run through the water, always against the wind. When sufficient momentum has been achieved, the huge bird soars into the sky and begins to flap its wings. This action is very much like an airplane when it takes off into the air by speeding down a runway.

When the albatross encounters strong winds and gales, the wings do not flap when it flies. Instead, the big bird glides for hours, low over the rolling seas.

The albatross lays its egg on remote, rocky, inaccessible islands. One white egg, four to five inches long, is produced. Both parents take turns sitting on the egg until it has hatched.

Sailors regard the albatross with great affection. They call the huge wandering albatross a gooney bird. The smaller birds they refer to as "mollyhawks" or "mallemucks." The sooty albatross (so-called because of its color), which flies over the waters of the Antarctic Circle, they have nicknamed the "quaker bird."

The albatross becomes quite tame. Sailors, by using salt pork for bait, are able to catch them with a hook and line, and haul them aboard the vessel. But they do not keep them on the ship for long. The albatross gets seasick from the roll of the ship. That's rather funny—a bird that spends most of its life flying over the ocean in all sorts of weather getting seasick! Albatrosses cannot take flight from the deck of a ship, so the sailors have to toss them overboard where they can run through the water and get back into the air.

Sailors also have the superstition that killing an albatross brings bad luck. The famous poem "Rime of the Ancient Mariner" by Samuel Taylor Coleridge was based on this superstition and made the albatross famous.

Misunderstood Mephitis
By A. A. Howe

One of the most entertaining and friendly of all the wood-folk animals is also the bravest. He has no fear of man or beast, and is greatly respected by all animals.

He is one of the farmer's best friends because he is a pest destroyer. He knows how to dance and play games. He and his family "march" in an orderly single file. He never provokes a fight. He is easily tamed and makes a lovely pet. Yet in spite of all this he is the most misunderstood of all animals. Scientists refer to him as *Mephitis mephitis*, but most everyone else knows him as the common or striped skunk. The common skunk has several relatives in the United States.

A French naturalist described this animal as "a beast of powerful scent." Actually this isn't quite true. It is not the smell of the animal itself, but the weapon it uses to defend itself, which gives off such an acrid, overpowering odor.

The skunk is a beautiful little animal, about cat size, weighing from eight to ten pounds. It has lustrous black fur, with a white patch on its forehead that spreads into two white streaks which run along its back, down to the tail. The tail is most remarkable, being almost as long as the body of the animal. It is very fine-haired, unusually bushy, and nearly as broad as it is long, with a pure-white tip that trails behind like a feathery plume.

The skunk has very bright, black eyes set in a small head with a long, pointed muzzle. It has short legs, rather large paws with five incompletely divided toes, and very strong forefeet which it uses to catch some of its food.

The common skunk lives in an area from Hudson Bay in Canada to Guatemala in Central America. It lives in dens and burrows which are lined with dry leaves and matted grasses. The skunk usually remains in its burrow by day, coming out at dusk in search of food, but sometimes you may see one during the day.

Skunks eat all kinds of insects— grasshoppers, crickets, June bugs, and potato bugs—and sometimes field mice, all of which are enemies of the farmer. Occasionally it will raid a poultry house, but this is very rare. And such a raid is partially offset by the skunk "clearing away" some of the rats and mice.

In late April or May the baby skunks are born. From six to ten babies are born in a litter. The babies are very helpless and small. After seven or eight weeks they begin to walk in that peculiar waddling gait which is like a bear walk, and follow their mother among the daisies. The babies are not fretful like other young animals. The family lives together and hunts together peacefully.

When a baby skunk leaves his burrow, he begins at once to earn his own way. He eats his own weight in worms, insects, and bugs, several times a week. He learns how

to catch little green grass snakes with his heavy flat-soled paws. And he becomes skillful at catching bees and wasps, routing them out like bears do, by great scratchings. When the bees swarm out, he beats them to the ground with his strong forefeet.

When skunks travel or go hunting, they have the curious habit of waddling in single file. Sometimes they stop to play.

Not many people have seen skunks at their play. They have a game which sometimes starts at early dusk. Five or more of the animals will form a circle with their noses pointed toward the center. Then they begin a sort of ceremonial dance. With their magnificent tails held high, they all move together at the same time with stiff-legged hops toward the center of the circle and advance till their noses touch. A moment later they retreat with the same stiff-legged, prancing gait to the outside of the circle. They act out this grotesque ritual a dozen times. Each time each move is the same. It is all done like clockwork.

When a skunk meets an enemy, such as a farmer's dog, immediately he follows by instinct an unusual behavior pattern. First he eyes the dog. It would be better for everyone if the dog would just go away.

But the dog advances, barks, and growls.

Then the skunk lowers his striped head, arches his back, and thumps his forefeet on the ground. Although this sound is not terrifying, the wild wood-folk understand and quickly run for cover.

But the dog doesn't understand, and charges again.

Patiently the skunk waits, making no move to challenge the dog. Standing stock-still, the skunk stares straight ahead, then very slowly shakes his head from side to side. It is an odd gesture, as if he were saying, "No, no, no."

The dog, still mystified, continues to growl and advance.

Now the skunk gracefully lifts his beautiful tail straight over his back. Then in a flash he turns and presents his rear to the dog, while at the same time arching his back. There is a sudden convulsive movement, then a thin jet of yellowish liquid glimmers brightly in the summer dusk. An acrid burning odor saturates earth and leaves, and drifts for hundreds of yards around.

The dog, yelping in agony, runs off. Never again will he trifle with a skunk. His hide has been drenched

with the sulphide that scientists call "mercaptan" which is secreted in glands under the skunk's tail. The spray has hit the dog in the eyes and has been inhaled in his lungs, and for a day or two he will be in misery.

This is what happens when a skunk is forced to fight. You can understand why it does not happen very often.

When the first snow falls, the skunk begins to eat much more and gets very fat. Later he remains inside his burrow. The snow chokes the entrance, sealing out the cold. His mother and brothers are there, too, and usually a couple of friends as well. They all lie curled together, without a sound, having their winter sleep. About mid-March, impulse and instinct awaken them.

Now it is time for the skunk to hunt for a mate. He ventures forth and finds her. He remains faithful. Then he hunts again, this time with his own family. The cycle continues year after year.

Chicago, our second largest city, has been named after him from the Indian word *segaku* which means "skunk" or "powerful."

It is a pleasure to know such an amiable and friendly creature as *Mephitis*. He is dedicated to peace, prefers the simple life, and asks only to be treated kindly, using his weapon only for defense.

Charlie Chipmunk

By Frances J. Chimenti

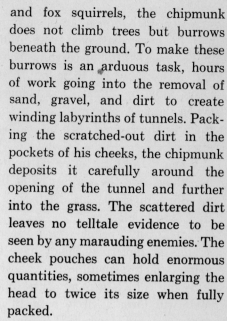

The word "hoarder" usually brings to mind a selfish, stingy miser. Yet if the chipmunk were not a hoarder, he would starve.

This tiny creature, half the size of a squirrel and a member of the same rodent family, finds it necessary to gather and store acorns and hickory nuts through late spring and summer, for he is desperately hungry when he awakes in the early spring after a long winter sleep. He eats up this hoard of nuts; then he has to spend the rest of spring and summer getting in a new supply for the coming winter.

You can catch sight of a chipmunk if you look for a streak of reddish-brown striped fur about five to six inches long with a four-inch slender tail.

The eastern chipmunk (*Tamias striatus*), also called the ground squirrel, is a native of the eastern United States and southeastern Canada. It has relatives that occur in the western United States and Canada, and eastern Asia.

Unlike his cousins, the red, gray, and fox squirrels, the chipmunk does not climb trees but burrows beneath the ground. To make these burrows is an arduous task, hours of work going into the removal of sand, gravel, and dirt to create winding labyrinths of tunnels. Packing the scratched-out dirt in the pockets of his cheeks, the chipmunk deposits it carefully around the opening of the tunnel and further into the grass. The scattered dirt leaves no telltale evidence to be seen by any marauding enemies. The cheek pouches can hold enormous quantities, sometimes enlarging the head to twice its size when fully packed.

The chipmunk eats sufficiently, while busily foraging for food, to maintain his health during the winter hibernation. Curled up in his burrow deep in the ground, his small body rises and falls in the soft breathing of deep slumber. He has many burrows, but the one he chooses for sleep is where he has accumulated the store of nuts.

During pioneer days, the chipmunk was a quarry for hunters or trappers because its meat was sweet and the fur soft and pliant. There may have been occasions when the children made pets of them, keeping them in a cage like white mice. Yet the true beauty of any living thing is when it is free, roaming its own natural habitat.

At the New York Botanical Garden civilization has come to the chipmunk. He has found that acorns and hickory nuts are his after much hard hunting and outwitting the rival squirrels, crows, and jays. He can get peanuts, too.

We have a favorite chipmunk at the Garden whom we call Charlie. We visit him quite often at his home in the Rock Garden section. From early spring until late fall he is visited by so many human

R. Kray

friends that his supply of peanuts must be quite extensive. He is a friendly fellow with us, but will have nothing to do with his cousins, the squirrels, who often get in his way. Charlie is what you might call a loner. A very busy creature, he races so quickly on his many errands that you almost miss his flight. Still, if you love the chipmunk as much as I do, you will always spot him.

We know that chipmunks usually make their homes under the roots of oak trees, the tunnel openings carefully hidden behind tufts of grass. However, our special Charlie has made a series of holes down into the earth between the rocks and stones in the Rock Garden.

At first we see only the lovely flowering plants and the trickle of the water over the helter-skelter varicolored rocks. We call, "Charlie! Charlie!" and rustle the bags of peanuts. Without a whisper or warning, there he is at our feet, ready for any gifts he can get.

I am the nearest. I crouch, and the tiny, furry animal-person creeps toward me. He poises bravely on the cement walk, his thin, fuzzy, reedlike tail quivering in eagerness. He raises little paws, so like human hands, before his chest and waits breathless, his unblinking eyes fastened on the bags of nuts.

"Here, Charlie, here is your peanut!" And he takes it, turns it over and over in his animal fingers, then pops it into one side of his mouth. He waits until another peanut comes out of the bag to be snatched and popped into the other side of his mouth. Sometimes he insists on waiting for a third peanut to be stuffed into whatever space is left in his cheeks.

On rainy days the Garden is silent. No one is about. We think of Charlie, warm and dry, nestled comfortably deep in his burrow, and it teaches us something. Here we are in our raincoats, rain dripping off the ends of our noses, but Charlie has the good sense to stay home!

The weather changes, the air grows chill; summer is ending. Charlie seems to know autumn is approaching and soon will come the time of hibernation. His anxious greed for the peanuts is quite apparent as he loses all fear, clambers up our arms, and plucks the peanuts from our fingers. A peanut is held a little too tightly. Charlie swings himself up onto the hand and clutches it, biting at the peanut for

a firmer hold, until he gets it.

In his frenzy and haste of grabbing the nuts and dashing off to hide them, Charlie becomes a little confused. He clutches my third finger as though it were a peanut, and gives a quick nibble. The finger must not have tasted like a peanut because he leaps back and runs for the bushes.

In a short time he recovers. Here he is again; more peanuts, bumpy stuffed cheek pockets. With a cheerfully brisk flirt of his skinny tail, Charlie darts off with swift grace and down into one of his tunnels to wherever it ends in a chipmunk's house.

Back he comes, ready for more. Again the same thing takes place, and away he darts. For as long as there are peanuts in the bag, Charlie will return. Somehow he knows when he has had the last peanut, and he makes small chittering noises to us that sound like "Thanks a lot, thanks a lot."

Whenever we come to the Garden, there is our Charlie. It is true that we are not absolutely certain if it is the same Charlie. But whichever one it is, we know he is our friend, new or old.

Did You Know?

Animals can talk, too! Of course it's animal talk. It's used to communicate between animals of the same type. Recently scientists have found that little dolphins, porpoises, and big whales have an exceedingly wide range of sounds that are used like a language.

A bear doesn't hibernate. The real trick of hibernation is the lowering of body temperature. During the winter a bear merely sleeps while his body temperature only drops by three or four degrees, not enough for true hibernation.

Dragon of the Sky

By Melvin I. Goldfarb

There is a monster loose in the land, a throwback to the dinosaur age. Born beneath the waves, he has learned to fly so well he can even stand still in mid-air. When he is hungry, which is most of the time, he can eat his own weight in food in a surprisingly short time. He is a fearsome yet beautiful sight, a killer of mosquitoes and flies, and a friend of man. He is the familiar insect, the dragonfly.

Have you ever watched a dragonfly hovering in the air? He is an impressive sight with his wings beating so rapidly and steadily that you can hardly see them. His huge eyes, each containing 15,000 lenses, assure him extremely keen sight. Once he detects the movement of a flying mosquito, he can suddenly accelerate to speeds as high as thirty miles per hour and swerve off after his prey.

Perhaps, as many people do, you call dragonflies "darning needles." They have no needles with which to darn, however, nor can they "sew up" a child's mouth. That's just an old story. In fact, they have no stingers with which to sting, and their needle-sharp teeth work only on other insects. They are entirely harmless to people.

The dragonfly is so much at home in the sky that the female will often lay her eggs while in flight. She will dart through the air just above the surface of a pond. Every so often she will dip her tail into the water, leav-

ing behind a cluster of eggs. Each cluster is encased in a gelatin-like substance which dissolves in the water. The eggs soon sink to the bottom of the pond where they usually hatch in about two or three weeks.

Other kinds of dragonflies have a second method of laying eggs. The female of some species will crawl down the stem of a water plant until she is completely submerged. She then cuts a slit in the plant stem and presses her eggs into it. While underwater, the dragonfly must have oxygen to breathe, just as you and I. If you are lucky enough to see a dragonfly go diving, you will notice a silvery bubble about it while it is underwater. This is a bubble of air which clings to its body and which it breathes while submerged.

The eggs of a dragonfly hatch into nymphs, a growing-up stage of many insects. Dragonfly nymphs live in warm water and cold, in streams and in stagnant ponds, in temperate zones and in the tropics. They have gills that are within the rear part of the digestive tract. Water is drawn into this part of the body, and the nymphs get the oxygen they need from this water. A nymph can expel the water strongly from its body, and, if it does this, it is driven forward somewhat like a rocket. The dragonfly nymph can move rapidly from one place to another in this way.

Like the adult dragonfly, the nymph is a hungry fellow. He lies in wait, camouflaged by his gray-green color, until some water bug or mosquito larva swims within range. Then his lower lip shoots out like a hand to grab his victim and thrust it into his mouth. Pincers at the end of this strange "hand" hold the victim tightly. The entire action is so swift that it is hard to follow even if

R. Knay

you are feeding nymphs in an aquarium.

The change of a nymph into an adult dragonfly is an amazing spectacle. When the times comes, usually after a year or two spent in the water, the nymph climbs onto the shore, a stick, or a weed. He pushes and pulls until his hardened outer layer of skin starts to split. His wet crumpled wings fall out into the warm air and start to unfold. Slowly the rest of him emerges from his old skin. In the warm sun, his wings soon dry and harden. Soaring through the sky, his wings beat the air as many as thirty times a second. He is no longer a creature of the water. He has suddenly become an accomplished flyer!

Food is ever on the mind of the adult dragonfly. Winging through the air, he folds his spine-covered legs in front of him to form a basket. In this manner he is able to scoop up his prey and devour it without having to halt his flight. Darting quickly back and forth through the air, he picks off flies and mosquitoes, seldom resting between each quick snack.

But as is often the case, the hunter is also the hunted. Birds love to pluck an unsuspecting dragonfly from the air. Frogs adore them, and the dragonfly that skims the surface of a trout-filled pond often winds up inside a trout.

Two hundred million years ago, dinosaurs walked the earth. Enormous flying reptiles with twenty-five-foot wingspans soared through the air in search of prey. Dragonflies the size of small hawks flew through the steaming air of prehistoric jungles, perhaps alongside of those huge ancient reptiles. The dinosaurs and flying reptiles are long gone, but the dragonfly remains. He has changed little, except in size.

Some kinds of dragonflies are bright-green, others red, some yellow, and some are copper-colored. Some are very small, but others have wingspans of almost seven inches. Next time you go fishing or are near a pond or stream, watch the dragonflies closely. If you can catch one, hold him by the wings and feed him an insect with a pair of tweezers. Watch how he eats it. Notice how his large head on its special joint easily turns in search of prey. If you see a dragonfly climb down a plant into the water, wait until she surfaces and flies away. Then take the stem of the plant home with you in a jar of pond water. Soon nymphs will hatch from eggs left in the stem. Or you might be able to catch some

nymphs by using a net. Place them in a fish tank filled with water from wherever you caught them and feed them. These are just a few of the ways in which you can observe these strange creatures of the water and air, living reminders of the age of dinosaurs.

Boy to Cardinal: "How do I know if you're a boy or a girl?"

Boy Cardinal: "Look at me. My colors are brighter and my tail is longer."

Girl Cardinal: "Showoff! Boasting of your colors has made your voice harsh. Mine is soft and sweet, like my color."

polar bear

Winter in the Zoo

By Glendia Fulkerson

Have you ever wondered what happens to the animals and birds in zoos located where winters are long and often very cold? Some animals have long, thick fur that keeps them warm even on the coldest days. They can stay outdoors all winter long. But other animals cannot survive in the severe cold. They usually live in places where the climate is very warm. Their fur is not heavy enough to keep them warm when the snow falls. And many birds cannot live long in very cold weather.

When the weather turns cold, the zoo keeper brings the birds indoors first. The flamingo, with its bright colors and long pink legs, is put in a warm building or basement which becomes his winter home.

Another bird, the stork, is also brought indoors soon after the cold weather arrives. His feathers are not heavy enough to keep him warm outdoors. Storks often are born and live for a time in cold climates. But just before the snow begins, they fly to a warmer place for the winter. Then in the spring they return to the cooler climate.

Birds of many kinds are found in the zoo. One of the most unusual is also the meanest. He is known as the Andean condor (Vultur gryphus), and is one of the largest birds in the world. The condor is glossy black. The wing coverts are pale ivory-gray with a black median band. Around the neck is a ruff of soft white down. The head may be one of several colors and has no feathers. Condors usually live high up in the Andes Mountains. They feed on dead animals, but sometimes they will catch a living animal for food. In the zoo, the condor must be kept in a separate cage for the protection of the other birds.

Many animals can stay outside in the winter because they have thick fur. The snow leopard has a thick, spotted coat and a very long, furry tail. Because he is almost entirely white, he is called a snow leopard. The timber wolf, like the snow leopard, usually lives in a cold, snowy region. Many timber wolves are white, too, and cannot easily be noticed in the snow.

The bears, of course, can stay outdoors in winter. Some kinds of bears go inside their caves and sleep during cold winter days. Others have such heavy fur that they do not seem to feel the cold. For the polar bear, winter is the very best time of the year. He usually lives in the Arctic region on top of the world where there is snow and ice all year long. The polar bear is right at home in the heavy snow and cold.

A moose stays outside all winter, too. He likes a cold climate and often finds plenty to eat under the snow. The deer is related to the moose; and, like the moose, enjoys cold weather. Deer are found in many parts of our country where the winters are cold.

Other big animals that are brought to the zoo must stay indoors during the winter because they have never known cold weather. The lion comes from southern Asia or Africa where the weather is very warm. Tigers, too, come from warm climates on the other side of the world.

The home of the hyena is also in Africa and Asia. You may have heard the hyena laugh in a zoo you have visited. You can be sure that the hyena is happy when he is brought indoors during the cold weather. His gray spotted fur is not heavy enough to keep him warm outside.

squirrel monkeys

Andean condor

One of the favorite animals in the zoo is the monkey. Most monkeys have short hair that is not heavy enough to keep them comfortable outdoors in the winter. The zoo keeper catches them and puts them in warm cages inside the zoo. They swing from bar to bar, in the same way they play in the trees during the summer. Crowds of people often gather around the monkey cages to enjoy watching their play.

Alligators sleep all winter. The zoo keeper may say that they sleep all summer too! "The only time they don't sleep," one zoo keeper said, "is when they're hungry." The alligator has to be moved indoors when it turns cold. He might freeze in the ice and snow. In the fall the zoo keeper and his helpers walk very cautiously into the alligator's outdoor pen and grab his jaws to keep from being bitten. While the zoo keeper holds the alligator's mouth shut, the helper grasps the alliga-

tor's tail and helps to carry him to his warm cage. Inside the zoo the alligator can now enjoy sleeping, just as he does outdoors during the summer.

Someday soon the zoo keeper and his helpers will not have to move the animals and birds indoors and outdoors because of the weather. Zoos of the future will be heated and cooled to suit the needs of different animals and birds. The polar bear will live in a cold pen all year long, and the lions will be warm in their cages. All year long, too, children will be able to go to the zoo and see the animals and birds in their attractive homes. Monkeys will be swinging from jungle trees; flamingos will be standing in a pen that looks like a swamp; and the honey bear will be sitting in a tree licking honey from a bees' nest. Throughout the whole year, the home of these animals and birds will be inside the zoo.

The Roadrunner

By Myron Sartain

Down in the border country between the United States and Mexico, life is hard. The land is very hot and very dry. The sun shines fiercely almost every day. Trees are small, and they don't make much shade. Clouds come sometimes, but they never stay long—and they don't leave rain behind very often.

Many unusual animals live in these desert lands. Some of them have strange habits. But these habits, even if they do seem strange to us, make life in the desert easier for the animals themselves.

Would you like to take a peek into the private life of one of these animals and see how he lives? Okay!

Come along and I'll introduce him to you.

Our friend is a bird. But don't expect to see him flitting about in the sky or roosting in the taller cactus. This fellow spends most of his time on the ground. Most people call him the roadrunner. But those who really know and love him call him "paisano," which means "fellow countryman" or "compatriot."

The roadrunner is an amusing, even comical character about the size of a small chicken. His vest is made from light-tan fuzzlike feathers. His ragged coat of loose dark-brown feathers, sprinkled with white, seems to fit poorly. But those loose-fitting feathers protect him from the burning sun, and their color lets him hide easily from his enemies.

Birds can't smile or frown, but paisano has found a way to express his feelings just the same. That perky crest atop his head can be raised or lowered to any degree as if to say, "I'm curious" or "I'm annoyed" or "I'm surprised" or whatever else he might be thinking. A patch of bright-red-and-blue skin shows behind each eye when his crest is fully raised, making his feathers even more expressive.

Usually the roadrunner travels in a dogtrot, his body bobbing like a cork on a pond at each step. But even then his head and the tip of his foot-long tail always stay the same distance above the ground.

When he is in a hurry, his long neck and tail flatten out almost level with the ground, and he moves like an arrow, leaving behind strange X-shaped footprints. High-speed turns are easy because he uses his tail for balance and steering. And it works like a brake when he wants to stop suddenly.

"Why," you ask, "would a bird rather run than fly?" That's an easy question. Since the roadrunner eats the small, quick insects and animals of the desert—grasshoppers, lizards, mice, and rats—he must be quicker than they are or he goes hungry. Some of his food hides in or under the thorny desert brush and can't be seen easily from the air. So walking or running proves best for this bird.

Roadrunners are famous for their habit of racing with horses. That's how they got their name. But horse racing is more than sport for the roadrunner. It serves a practical purpose. The noise made by the horse, or any other large animal moving down the trail, frightens insects and small animals from their hiding places in the brush. As they try to escape, the clever roadrunner is there to gobble them up. Sometimes a lizard, the paisano's favorite food, tries to make its escape down the trail. But the roadrunner is too quick.

The lizards he catches are always swallowed headfirst, but some are too long to go all the way down. This doesn't bother the paisano. He just runs around with part of the lizard's tail hanging from his beak until more room is available in his stomach.

Would roadrunners go hungry if they had no horses to frighten in-

sects from their hiding places? No, indeed! This clever bird has another method of hunting. He walks very quietly through the desert brush, flicking his wings open, then closed. Insects and lizards are frightened from their cozy hideouts by the flash of the paisano's white wing tips.

Snails are a favorite item on the roadrunner's menu. "But snails have hard shells," you say. Don't worry. The wise paisano has a solution to that problem. He just taps the snail against a rock until its shell cracks open. And did you know that he always picks the same rock for that purpose? Each time he finds a snail, he walks back to this special rock. Sometimes he has to walk quite a distance, past many rocks that would work just as well. No one but paisano knows why he does it, and perhaps he himself has forgotten the reason.

Roadrunners have such big appetites that they will eat almost any of the horned, thorned, stinging, or biting creatures of the desert. This includes tarantulas, scorpions, bees, centipedes, and rattlesnakes.

Yes, even rattlesnakes! The roadrunner is the most famous rattle-snake killer in the Southwest. But some of the stories are just tall tales. They were made up by South-westerners to impress outsiders. Old-timers used to claim that paisano would build a cactus fence around a sleeping snake. When the snake woke up, the roadrunner would tease him into fighting. But each time he struck, the angry rattler would get a mouthful of cactus instead of paisano feathers. Finally the snake would get too tired to put up a good fight. The roadrunner would finish the battle with a few quick pecks on the snake's head. The story is amusing, but it is probably no more than legend. At least no scientist has seen it happen that way.

But roadrunners do kill rattle-snakes. People have even made movies of their combat. It's very exciting to watch the rattler coil, then strike at the bird. But the paisano is too quick. He just flicks his bony wings in the snake's face and dances aside in a cloud of dust. Sometimes the roadrunner stands his ground and pecks the snake's head very hard. The fight may last over half an hour. But finally the snake gets too tired to continue. The roadrunner dashes in, and the snake is finished.

So, you see, life in the desert can be very interesting and very exciting. And for characters like the roadrunner, there is never a dull moment.

Matching Birds

Look at each bird at the left.
Find the bird like it at the right.

The Squid
Jet-Propelled Ocean Trickster

By Myron Sartain

To the sailors in ancient times, the seas were sometimes frightening places. They did not know what kinds of animals lived in the ocean and naturally they wondered. Sailors returning from voyages told tales of "sea serpents" that wrestled with whales, of "devil fish" that sank small boats, and of long-armed monsters that snatched men from the decks of ships.

Scientists did not believe these tales. Stories are not proof. Then, during the years from 1870 to 1880, the scientific world got the proof it wanted. Fishermen began pulling the monsters from the deep oceans in their fishing nets.

People are not afraid of things they know and understand. The monsters turned out to be no more than giant cousins to the common squid that had been caught as food for hundreds of years along almost every coastline in the world.

Some of the stories told by the sailors turned out to be true. Scientists have decided that, even though they are seldom seen, the giant squid must be large enough to fight with sperm whales which feed upon them. Since the long, rubbery tenta-

cles of the giant squid do resemble huge snakes, it is easy to see how that version of the sea serpent stories got started. Giant squid are large enough to sink a small boat. Some of them are over sixty feet long and weigh several hundred pounds. But they are seldom seen at the surface of the oceans.

Even the smaller squid are interesting animals. There are about 350 species or kinds of squid, and they come in many sizes. Some full-grown squid are just two inches long. Most of the common squid are less than three feet long.

The common, or most frequently seen, squid lives in the open oceans. He is a fast, agile swimmer and is often seen flashing about like a small, glistening rocket, powered by his own special kind of jet propulsion. Water sucked in to provide air for his gills can be forced out through a funnel. Each squirt drives him several feet through the water at high speed.

The squid has ten very flexible arms attached directly to his head. His body is attached to the other side of his head. It is long and tapered like a torpedo, giving him a

streamlined shape for high-speed swimming. At the very tip he has two small fins which help him with balance and steering. He uses them sometimes when he wants to swim slowly. But when he is really in a hurry, he seems to be swimming backwards with his arms trailing out behind.

Two of the common squid's rubbery arms are longer than the other eight. They are called tentacles, and he whips them out to catch his lunch as it swims nearby. Powerful suction cups lined with hooks like cats' claws cover the pawlike ends of the two tentacles, keeping a firm hold on slick, wiggling prey. Then the eight arms wind around the prey, gripping tightly with their suckers, and pull the food to the squid's sharp parrot-like beak.

Life is not always easy for the squid. He seems to be the favorite item on everyone's menu. He is often pursued by porpoises, whales, seals, penguins, and many others, including man himself. But the squid has several ways to avoid being eaten. He is agile and quick enough to dodge larger enemies. The two large, bright eyes that decorate his head are constructed much like our eyes, and he probably can see as well as we.

Certain species of squid can even fly when they wish. They do so by racing through the water, pumping madly with their jet funnels, then bursting out of the water to glide fifty or sixty yards through the air. The less-able common squid often skips along the water's surface to escape enemies.

A special trick helps the squid avoid becoming the main dish at someone's dinner party. As he jets away from danger, the squid dumps a dark cloud of special ink into the water. He himself instantly turns pale and becomes almost invisible. The ink cloud hides his escape. Sometimes it serves as a decoy to hold his enemy's attention while he scoots away. Imagine the confusion that occurs when an enemy rips into a school of squid. Each squid squirts away in a different direction, leaving behind an inky copy of himself. The enemy rushes here and there, attacking the cloudy shapes —while the squid head for safer waters.

A squid cannot imitate the many color shades and patterns of his relative the cuttlefish, but his ability to change colors when he wishes is useful in many ways to him.

Besides turning pale and invisible as a ghost to escape the attention of his enemies, the squid can blend almost perfectly with his surroundings. When an unsuspecting fish swims too close, out flash his tentacles to grab supper. With his tummy full and no enemies in sight, the squid may rest for a few quiet minutes. At such times a smoky rainbow of color may ripple across his body, showing that he is happy with his world.

Porpoises

By Edward B. Tracy

Bottle-nose dolphins, commonly known as porpoises, are not fish but mammals and are among the best jumpers and fastest swimmers of all the creatures that live in the water.

During recent years people in the United States and several other countries have had the opportunity to become better acquainted with these friendly creatures as a result of seeing them perform in various aquariums and during some television programs. The patience and skill of some of the cleverest trainers have produced remarkable results with porpoises, and have proven that they possess an intelligence far beyond what some of the old sailors and fishermen considered remarkable.

There are about twenty different species of porpoises, ranging in length from three and one-half to over eight feet and weighing from sixty to four hundred and fifty pounds. Their home is mostly in the sea, but a few species are to be seen in fresh-water rivers.

The areas where they are found range from the Arctic to the South Pacific Oceans. They have been seen in the rivers of South East Asia, Malaysia, and hundreds of miles up the Amazon River.

Porpoises, like whales, breathe through a small hole in the top of their heads. Every few minutes they rise to the surface with part of their head out of water for a quick breath of air.

The shape of their bodies is one of nature's most perfect examples of streamlining. Porpoises propel themselves with an up-and-down movement of their wonderfully shaped tails. This is directly opposite from the way a fish swims by swishing its tail from side to side.

The tail movement of a porpoise in combination with its very flexible, sleek body and great strength accounts for the speed at which it can travel and its ability to leap for a distance of several times its own length when the occasion requires.

Probably the worst enemy of the porpoise is the killer whale, often

described as the wolf of the sea. They are much smaller than other species of whales but are the fiercest and the swiftest. They hunt in schools of four, or more, and it really taxes a porpoise's intelligence and speed to escape when he is surrounded by several of these killers.

bullfrog

What We Know About Frogs

By Steven C. Anderson

California Academy of Sciences

Out in the country, when the sun has gone down and the light is fading, the evening chorus begins. Prominent in the spring concert are the voices of frogs. Since most frogs must lay their eggs in water, a farm pond is often the center stage for this choir. It is only the male frogs who sing, and their serenade helps to guide other frogs to the breeding site. Each kind of frog has a characteristic voice, from the high soprano of some tree frogs to the low bass of the familiar bullfrog. So it is not hard for each lady frog to recognize an appropriate mate.

By sitting patiently near a pond at night with a flashlight, you will see that, as the frog sings, he inflates either one large or two small sacs like balloons under his throat. These sacs are filled with air which is forced back and forth over his vocal cords. It is surprising to find a very loud voice coming from a small tree frog, his vocal sac blown up larger than his head.

When the frogs have found mates, egg-laying begins. The male clasps the female with his front legs around her waist or chest while she lays her eggs. As the eggs are released, they are fertilized by the sperm which the male releases over them.

Collect a few of the eggs, and watch the first stages of a frog's life. Place the eggs in a large jar or pan of fresh pond water or water from the tap which has been allowed to stand overnight. When the eggs hatch in a few days, you will see that the babies don't look much like their parents.

During the first part of its life, the baby frog is called a tadpole. It swims about in the water, never coming onto land. It has a fishlike tail for swimming, and a small mouth, most unfroglike, for scrap-ing off tiny pieces of algae and water plants which form its diet. After a time, small hind legs start to grow. Finally, the front legs break through openings in the skin. The tail becomes shorter and shorter as the young frog's body absorbs it.

At last the change is complete. A second life has begun. The frog now is a small edition of his parents. From now on he will spend much of his time on land and eat only live food, mostly insects. It is best for you to let your frog go to find his own meals.

There is a great difference in the time it takes for different kinds of frogs to change from tadpole to frog. The spadefoot toads, which lay their eggs in temporary ponds formed by the rain, pass through their tadpole life in a few weeks, while the bullfrog may stay a "baby" for two years.

Frogs have been around for millions of years. And during that time gradual changes in their bodies and habits have occurred, resulting in hundreds of kinds of frogs, some of which are able to live in unexpected places.

In the tropics, pools are often small, and there are many animals that love to dine on frog eggs and tasty tadpoles. Some frogs have an advantage in being able to care for their eggs and babies. The male Surinam toad, for example, presses the fertilized eggs into the spongy skin of his wife's back. There they hatch, and the tiny frogs develop in little pockets, finally popping out of small lids in Mama's skin. The marsupial frog, a member of the tree frog family, has a pouch on her back for carrying the eggs. In Argentina there lives a strange frog called the "vaquero." Papa does the baby-sitting; he carries the developing tadpoles in his vocal sac until metamorphosis is complete and the young frogs are ready to care for themselves. These and other frogs have lost the need for water always at hand, and some have done away entirely with the tadpole part of their lives. Other frogs build "nests" of various kinds, either in or out of the water, to protect their eggs. Such frogs generally lay fewer eggs, but a greater percentage live to grow up.

Some frogs live in places where there are no permanent streams or ponds. The adult frogs must dig beneath the surface of the ground and stay where it is moist during the dry seasons. Often such frogs carry their own shovels—strong, sharp little spades on their hind feet. Some frogs spend their whole lives in such protected places as termite nests, where their dinner is always on the table. There are even a few frogs which develop a cellophane-like covering over their whole bodies during dry periods, which prevents

spring peeper

them from drying out. When it rains, the frogs come out and lay their eggs in the temporary pools and puddles. The tadpoles then develop very quickly before the ponds dry up.

Part of the reason frogs can live in so many different places is that they have evolved many ways of avoiding enemies. One way is a quick, long jump into the water.

Members of the tree frog family, which includes the familiar spring peepers, are very acrobatic, able to leap from one small twig to another.

Toads, those common residents of backyards and gardens, rely for protection on the fact that most animals do not consider them tasty. Chemicals in the skin not only make them taste bad, but also make them poisonous to eat. Toads live throughout all of the continents except Australia and Antarctica.

In tropical America the "poison arrow frogs" advertise their presence in brilliant yellows, reds, and metallic greens. The poison of their skin is so powerful that the Indians use it on their arrows. When a bird or small animal is shot with such an arrow, the poison paralyzes it very quickly.

Other frogs depend for their safety on their ability to hide. They have colors and patterns of green and brown which make them hard to see in the light and shadow of the forest.

Frogs live in tropical rain forests, in deserts, and up to 15,000 feet high in the Himalaya Mountains of Asia. A few live as far north as the Arctic Circle and others as far south as Patagonia.

By studying frogs, biologists have learned a great deal about evolution, growth, and development, and the many ways animals are able to "make a living." The distribution of the many frog families even gives us a clue to the past history of the earth and its changing climates and geography. Perhaps the most fascinating thing about the study of frogs is that there is still so much we do not know about them!

tadpole development

emu

lacewing

guillemot

hummingbird

wheel bug

lizard

ostrich

tinamou

nightjar

oyster catcher

kingfisher

The Wonder of Eggs

By Ruth Jaeger Buntain

Every day, all over the world, millions, billions, and trillions of eggs are being laid. They are laid by all kinds of creatures, in all kinds of nests, in all kinds of places.

Some of these eggs are so small they can only be seen through a microscope. Others are so large they look like baseballs. The eggs of most insects are no larger than pencil points. The eggs of hummingbirds are about the size of peas. Those of the ostrich are about seven inches long.

Eggs are of many shapes. They are round, cone-shaped, oblong, pear-shaped, and pebble-shaped.

Some eggs look like beads. Some look like bunches of grapes. An insect called the lacewing lays eggs that look like the buds of flowers. Those of the wheel bug are shaped like round bottles.

The eggs of some birds that nest in high, open places are shaped like cones and there is little danger of rolling off and breaking. The guillemot lays an egg of such a shape. She lays it on the stony shelf of a high sea cliff. Because of its shape, it can roll only in a small circle.

The eggs of the nightjar, a bird which lays its eggs on the ground, look like small pebbles. Their ap-

pearance keeps them from being bothered.

Eggs differ in the kind of shells they have. There are thin shells and thick shells; soft shells and hard shells. The eggs of most lizards are thick and leathery. The egg of the kingfisher is so thin that light can be reflected through it.

The eggs of sharks are protected by a horny shell. These have long tendrils that cling to rocks and seaweeds, and prevent the eggs from drifting ashore.

Eggs are of many colors. The emu's eggs are green. The robin's are blue. Those of the wild turkey are cream-white with red dots. The mockingbird's are bluish-green with brown specks. The eggs of the tinamou are among the wonders of bird life. They are so highly burnished that they look like gleaming bits of porcelain.

Eggs that are laid in holes or hollows of trees, such as the owl's and the woodpecker's, are usually white. Those that are laid in places that are not sheltered are colored with spots and streaks and often blend into the background. The oyster

catcher, a bird of the seacoast, lays its eggs in the sand. They are colored buff and are streaked with dark brown, looking like the sand on which they lie.

The eggs of most birds which nest in the early spring, among trees and bushes, are of greenish hue. Their color blends into the foliage, and they are largely undetected by egg-eating animals.

Eggs are found in many different places: on craggy cliffs, on the bottom of the ocean, on the burning sands of the desert, and on the frozen shores of the Arctic Ocean. Some birds, such as the grebe, build nests on floating pieces of marsh plants. Others, like the house wren, sometimes nest in tin cans and in the pockets of coats. The dipper, or water ouzel, often builds its nest in the spray of cataracts, and sometimes behind them. The eggs of the midwife toad are carried about on the legs of the male.

Sometimes there is just one egg

in a nest. The puffin, the noddy tern, and the murre are single-egg-laying birds. So is the petrel, a water-walking bird. Unlike most birds, the male petrel incubates the egg during the daytime while the female is searching for food. When night comes, the female takes her turn on the nest and the male disappears until morning.

Penguins use no kind of nest for their solitary egg. The emperor penguin incubates it on top of his webbed feet, beneath a flap of skin. The incubation period lasts through the subzero Antarctic winter.

Sometimes there are just a few eggs in a nest. Hummingbirds invariably lay two. Plovers usually lay four. Robins lay four or five. Most wild birds lay from four to eight, although a few lay as many as twenty. The ostrich lays about ten.

Sometimes there are hundreds and thousands of eggs in a nest. Certain fish such as the cod, sturgeon, and turbot, whose eggs are eaten by hundreds of enemies, lay millions of eggs. A single oyster may produce as many as 500 million eggs a year. Only a small number, however, will escape the egg-eating animals that are waiting for a meal.

In mammals, with the exception of the echidna and the platypus, the eggs do not leave the body of the mother. These do not have shells because they do not need to be protected. They stay inside the mother's body where they are nurtured and kept warm until it is time for the living young to be born. This is the way it is with human eggs—eggs that are so small they can hardly be seen by the human eye. The egg remains in the mother's womb until the life it has cradled is ready to live outside her body. Then the miracle of birth takes place.

Whatever the size, shape, or color of eggs, and regardless of where they are found, how many are laid, or how they are hatched, eggs are the most wonderful things in all the world. For an egg contains the germ of life, and every egg is the beginning of a living creature.

Did You Know?

An earthworm doesn't breathe through a mouth or nose like you; he breathes through his skin.

A deer gets a new set of antlers every year. During the winter his old set begins to get itchy and he rubs them against trees until they come off. If you see him early in the spring, he won't have any antlers at all!

Birds have a calendar, too. Birds have a special way of telling how long the days are. When the days get shorter in the fall, they know it is time to go south. And when the days get longer in the spring, it is time to come back. It took scientists a long time to learn this secret, and they still do not know everything about it.

Although some dinosaurs were pretty big, the blue whale is bigger and heavier than all of them.

A hummingbird's wings buzz because he beats them more than five thousand times each minute. If you could flap your arms that fast, you would buzz, too.

A beaver sharpens his own teeth. The outside of each tooth is softer than the center of it, so the softer part wears off first, leaving the harder part always sharp.

A fish can't see as far as you can. But, he can point his eyes in two directions at once!

If a bird doesn't have any teeth, how can he chew? He swallows his food whole and his gizzard grinds it.

A catfish has fingers. Well, not really, but he uses his whiskers to touch and feel the bottom of a murky lake just as we might use our hands.

A bird stays on a perch when asleep because of the automatic lock mechanism in his feet.

emperor penguin

midwife toad

robin

shark

cod

The Belted Kingfisher:
A Bird That Fishes

By Luther F. Addington

One summer day I sat beside a pool of a small mountain stream. Suddenly a big-headed bird with a scraggly topknot, a big bill, and a short tail, swooped down to a branch of a maple tree which extended over the pool. It was a kingfisher, a bird slightly larger than a robin.

Its upper part was of a grayish-blue color. A white collar circled its neck. Its throat was also white except for the two breast-bands crossing it. It had white spots in front of its eyes and white tips on its wings. But its belly was a chestnut color which told me, along with the double breast-bands, that it was a hen.

There she sat, looking down as if to say she could beat me catching fish. And she made a loud rattling sound which showed that I had disturbed her.

Well, that big-headed bird suddenly made a nose dive into the water and quickly came up with a beating of wings which seemed to knock every drop of water from its feathers. With a four-inch-long chub in its strong black beak, it perched on the same maple branch. In a moment it tossed the fish into the air, caught it by the head, and swallowed it.

It surely swallowed the fish in the right way. The fish wouldn't have gone down its throat tail-first because the fins would have caught in its mouth.

It gave one more rattling sound as if to make fun of my failure to catch a fish, then winged away upsteam. Quickly I drew my field glasses from their leather case and watched. A short way upstream it lighted on a sandy bank on the other side of the stream.

Leaving my rod and reel, I stole among the bushes to a point opposite the sandy bank. Again I lifted my field glasses. I located Mrs. Kingfisher at once. In a moment I saw dirt flying out of a small hole in the bank near her. Soon another kingfisher appeared at the mouth of the hole. This one had but one band on its breast, and its underpart was white. These were the markings of the papa kingfisher.

I knew what he was doing: digging a tunnel. From past observation I knew the papa would keep digging until the tunnel extended from six to nine feet into the bank. At the end of the tunnel he'd scratch out a room in which the mama would lay her eggs.

I saw the papa give the little mound of dirt at the tunnel entrance a swipe with his four-toed foot. His third and fourth toes are welded together and make his foot a good dirt shoveler.

Whenever I could, I watched to see what would happen to the kingfisher family. Then one day I saw eight baby birds come out with the mother. Both the mama and papa brought minnows and fed their young. Later on all the kingfishers, old and young, flew away.

Then I dug the dirt away from the tunnel. At the end of it I found a small room. It had a fishy smell. That was easily understood, for the nest was on a bed of fish bones. Kingfishers do not digest the bones of the fish they swallow. They spit them up after the meat is digested.

And what do these birds in the north do in winter when streams freeze over and they can't dive for fish? Well, they're smart. They fly south where there is no ice, and continue to earn their living by fishing.